ACTIVITY BANK

Alcohol

Terry Brown

Contents

Editor: Emma Ray
Layout artist: Patricia Hollingsworth
Illustrations: Dandi Palmer (page 45), Sarah Wimperis – Graham-Cameron Illustration

© 2000 Folens Limited, on behalf of the author.

Every effort has been made to contact copyright holders of material used in this book. If any have been overlooked, we will be pleased to make any necessary arrangements.

First published 2000 by Folens Limited, Dunstable and Dublin.

Folens Limited, Albert House, Apex Business Centre, Boscombe Road, Dunstable, LU5 4RL, England.

ISBN 1 86202 565–7

Printed in Singapore by Craft Print.

How to use this book

There are 22 activities contained within this book. Each one has a teacher instruction page and a pupil activity page. The activities can be completed in short time slots or extended into longer periods, depending on the length of time you have available. They can also be differentiated to suit the needs of less able pupils. The activities can be presented in any order and you do not have to work your way right through the book. A matrix on page 48 provides a useful summary of, and reference to, the skills that pupils will learn through each activity, but we do recommend that Activity 1 and Activity 2 are delivered as a starting point to your series of lessons and Activity 22 as a review at the end.

Most of the activities in this book need few materials or resources other than copies of the activity sheet, paper and pens. They are designed to keep the teacher's workload to a minimum beyond planning how each activity will be carried out in the classroom. Most are designed so that pupils can work individually, in pairs or in small groups, depending on the teacher's preference. We recommend a balance of whole class, small group and individual work to provide pupils with plenty of opportunity to express their views, to listen and to try to understand the views of others and to develop communication and social skills.

The aims and expected outcomes of each activity are clearly indicated and the format for all activities is consistent to enable you quickly to feel comfortable and familiar with the style. All the information a teacher needs is contained here, not only to present the lesson confidently, but also to answer most questions that arise.

Introduction

Most young people will have their first taste of alcohol between 11 and 16 years of age. Alcohol is the socially acceptable and legal drug of choice for most of modern western society. However, it can cause a lot of problems, both to those who drink it and for others who have to deal with the consequences. *Activity Bank: Alcohol* intends to assist the pupils with this situation by providing them with accurate information about the laws and facts relating to alcohol. The group activities will help them to consider their own and other people's attitudes to alcohol and to develop a responsibility towards making decisions relating to their health and personal well-being.

The content of this pack is based on an adaptation of the example drug education programme detailed in *Drug Education: Curriculum Guidance for Schools* (SCAA/DfEE 1995) and covers the alcohol education element in the Scottish Office Education Department National Guidelines for Health Education.

Alcohol education should be included in drug education, which should be an integral part of Personal, Social and Health Education lessons. The pupils' education about alcohol is best delivered in the context of a clear policy outlining procedures for dealing with situations involving alcohol, which has been developed in consultation with governors, parents, pupils and relevant external agencies.

Teachers will also need to be aware of the sensitivities of the pupils' cultural and religious backgrounds when planning their lessons.

The effect of alcohol abuse on health features in the *Life and Living Processes* attainment target in the National Curriculum Science Programme of Study. Before embarking on the activities in this book, consultation with the Science Department may elicit the information covered in Science lessons, and possibly promote coordination and reinforcement.

Message in a bottle

Pupil consultation

AIMS

To assess the pupils' needs to ensure that they are covered in future lessons.

Teaching Points

- ◆ It is important that the alcohol education lessons are relevant to the level of knowledge, needs and concerns of the pupils and therefore they need to be consulted about it.
- ◆ It is intended, through the anonymity of the responses, to encourage an open and honest reaction from the pupils to ensure that the rest of the lessons meet their real needs.
- ◆ Keep the sheet generated in Step 3 for use in Activity 22.
- ◆ Use the information gathered by this activity to inform curriculum planning to ensure that, as far as possible, the alcohol education lessons meet the pupils' needs.

USING THE ACTIVITY SHEET

The focus of the activity is to draw out the thoughts and attitudes of the pupils before planning future lessons, in order to produce a more effective series of lessons.

Step 1   Explain to the pupils that this activity is intended to find out what they think is important for this series of lessons on alcohol education, so that you can plan ahead to meet their needs. Hand out the activity sheet. This should be completed individually, honestly, anonymously and without discussion.

Step 2   In small groups, prepare a composite response on a large enough piece of paper for display and include a tally for items appearing more than once.

Step 3   Display all the sheets and complete a class version, seeking clarification if necessary. Ask the pupils to prioritise the list and tell them if there are any areas that you are not able to deal with. Otherwise, indicate that you will attempt to cover everything on this sheet in the lessons and will return to it at the end of the series to review progress.

Step 4   Ask the groups to discuss the whole activity of this lesson and to feed back three words to describe it.

Extension Activities

- ◆ Ask the pupils to use the questions on the activity sheet to consult their parents about what they think should be dealt with in a series of alcohol education lessons and compare it with the opinions of the class.
- ◆ Ask the pupils to choose one of the issues on the sheet to research in preparation for the lessons. Suggest that they use a library, the Internet or ask older people for information. The final results should be presented to the class.

Outcomes

- ◆ An interest in the subject encouraged by consulting the pupils about their needs.
- ◆ The start of the development of trust between the teacher and the pupils.
- ◆ An indication of the pupils' level of knowledge and their current needs.
- ◆ Development of collaboration and collation skills.

Message in a bottle

Write down your answers in the bottles below.

1. Alcohol – what I know.

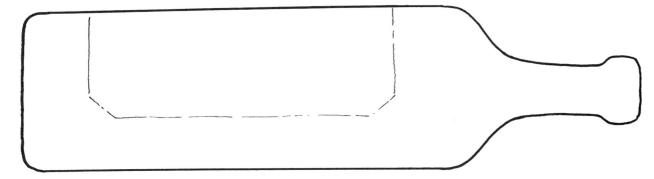

2. Alcohol – what I want to find out about.

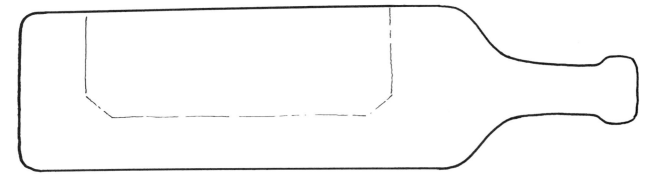

3. Alcohol – what my concerns are.

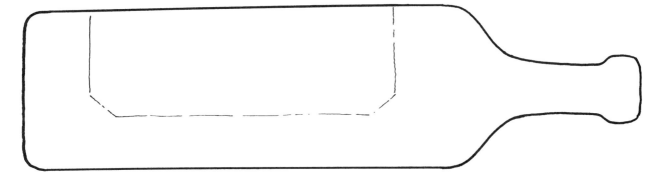

4. Alcohol education – what the teacher can do to help.

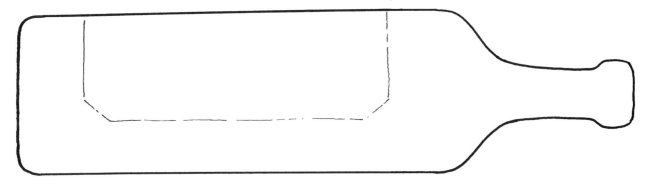

5. Circle the most important factors in each bottle.

ACTIVITY BANK: *Alcohol*

Ground rules

Enabling sensible discussion

AIMS

To generate ground rules to enable open and sensible discussion about alcohol.

Teaching Points

Materials needed
A large display version of a drinking glass.

- Explain to the pupils why it is important to establish ground rules.
- Make clear the school's position with regard to confidentiality, contact with parents and anything else that is appropriate for this subject.
- Rules need to be agreed by all, including you, before writing them up.
- Rules that may be suggested include: one person to speak at a time; an individual's right to express and not to express an opinion; protection from questions about personal experience, including those of the teacher.
- The teacher can contribute relevant rules if the pupils miss them out.
- In order for the rules to work, the teacher must keep to them as well.

USING THE ACTIVITY SHEET

The focus of the activity is to explore the problems of discussing alcohol and to agree on a framework in which the issues can be dealt with openly, honestly and non-judgementally.

Step 1 Tell the class that you want to develop a classroom atmosphere that will enable everyone to feel comfortable discussing alcohol. Hand out copies of the activity sheet. Ask the pupils, individually and without discussion, to write down, outside the glass, anything they think would get in the way of an open and helpful classroom discussion.

Step 2 Ask the pupils, in small groups, to share these hindrances and come up with ways to counter them, writing them inside the glass.

Step 3 Take one suggestion from each group and negotiate acceptance of it with the whole class. Write it up on your own display version of a drinking glass. Do the same with others the groups suggest.

Step 4 Ask members of the class what they think of these rules – if they can keep to them, what to do if they are broken, and what they think of the process of developing them. Request a title for the poster. Display it at the beginning of each lesson.

Extension Activities

- Ask the pupils to compare why and how these rules were created with another set of rules or laws, such as school rules, age restrictions, the Highway Code, rules for sports and so on.
- They should compare these rules with ones that apply in formal situations, for example parliament, courts, police enquiries and so on. At the end of the exercise, ask them to list the differences and similarities.

Outcomes

- A set of ground rules to facilitate open, sensible discussion about alcohol, which everyone in the class has agreed upon and that they all have an interest in maintaining.
- Some understanding of the need for consensus and how to reach it.

Ground rules

1. Write outside the glass the things that would get in the way of a sensible class discussion about alcohol.

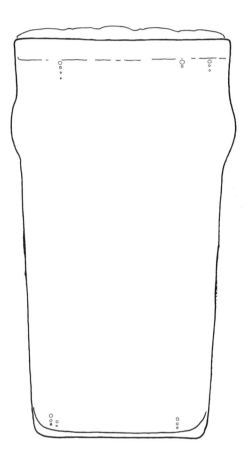

2. In your group, discuss and write down, inside the glass, what the members of the class, including the teacher, could do to overcome these problems.

ACTIVITY BANK: *Alcohol*   7

School rules about alcohol

You need to know what they are

AIMS

To ensure the pupils know the school rules and procedures about alcohol.

Teaching Points

◆ Incidents involving alcohol should be dealt with by the school in a caring, fair and consistent manner.
◆ The pupils may not agree with all the school rules but have to accept them, unless there is a structure for consultation, for example a school council.
◆ School rules and procedures should cover: bringing alcohol to school, procedures for dealing with a pupil under the influence of alcohol, sanctions, parental involvement and use of alcohol on the school premises by staff and visitors.

USING THE ACTIVITY SHEET

The focus of the activity is to enable the pupils to understand the school rules about alcohol and the reasons for them, starting with their own views.

Step 1   Tell the pupils that you want them to consider school rules about alcohol. Hand out the activity sheets and ask them, working individually, to write in the 'My home' drawing, the rules about alcohol in their home. Ask them to share the results in groups, without class feedback.

Step 2   In the same groups, discuss and decide upon rules and procedures about alcohol that would apply in their ideal school.

Step 3   Ask each group to feed back one of their rules. Discuss each one and its relation to your school rules. Write them on the board in two columns: ones that are the same as the school rules and those that are not. Explain the school rules and procedures about alcohol, and the reasons for them. Ask the pupils, working individually, to draw their school and to write the school rules inside their drawing.

Step 4   Ask the pupils, in groups, to compare the school rules with the ones they generated for their 'Ideal school', and to feed back one positive aspect of the school rules and one aspect they are not entirely happy with.

Extension Activities

◆ Ask the pupils to develop rules about alcohol that would apply in their 'Ideal home' and use an appropriate software package to produce a poster of them.
◆ Pupils should consider the similarities and differences between the school rules about alcohol and those about medicines, illegal drugs, dress, mobile phones and so on, and the reasons for them.

Outcomes

◆ An understanding of the school rules about alcohol and the reasons for them.
◆ An awareness that conventions about alcohol are different in different people's homes from those in school.
◆ An understanding that some rules may not be negotiable, and of the consequences of breaking them.

School rules about alcohol

1. Write or draw the rules about alcohol that apply in your home in the drawing below.

   My home

2. Share your rules with a small group.

3. In your small group, generate rules and procedures about alcohol that would apply in your ideal school.

   Ideal school

4. Draw an outline of your school and write the rules about alcohol inside your drawing.

   Our school

The laws about alcohol

Ignorance is no defence

AIMS

To ensure pupils know which alcohol laws apply to them.

Teaching Points

◆ The under 18 alcohol laws:

Under 5	May not be given alcohol except on medical orders.
5 plus	May drink alcohol at home, in registered private clubs or in any public place (subject to local by-laws).
Under 14	May not be present in the bar of licensed premises unless: accompanied by a person 18 years or older, it is before 9pm, or the bar has a children's certificate.
14 plus	May be in a bar of licensed premises during permitted hours.
16 plus	May buy beer, port, cider or perry (and wine in Scotland) with a meal in an eating area in licensed premises.
Under 18	May not purchase, be supplied with, or consume alcohol in a bar.
	May not purchase alcohol from an off-licence or supermarket.
	May not be employed in a bar or licensed premises.
	In Northern Ireland only, may not enter licensed premises.

USING THE ACTIVITY SHEET

The focus of the activity is to compare the pupils' knowledge of the law with the reality, and to ensure that they are clear about the alcohol laws that apply to them.

Step 1 Tell the members of the class that you want to find out what they know about the age-related alcohol laws. Hand out copies of the activity sheet. Ask the pupils, working individually, to mark what they think they can legally do at which ages on the 'what do you think' time-line.

Step 2 Ask the pupils to compare what they have done with a partner or small group.

Step 3 Draw two time-lines on the board and, starting from birth, ask the pupils what they think

they can legally do at which ages, marking them on one of the time-lines. Then write the correct laws from the information box on the other time-line as you reach the appropriate age. Ask the pupils to write these laws on 'the law' time-line on their activity sheet.

Step 4 When all the laws have been covered, ask the pupils to compare their two time-lines and to feed back a law they knew correctly and the one that they did not know, that surprised them the most.

Extension Activities

◆ Ask the pupils to devise a chart comparing the alcohol laws with laws for other activities, such as driving, films, loans, sex and so on.
◆ The pupils should prepare a questionnaire to ask the people at home what they think the laws are about alcohol. Compare the results with the reality.

Outcomes

◆ A specific knowledge of the age-related alcohol laws.
◆ An awareness that some laws are there to protect young people.

The laws about alcohol

What do you think you can do at which age?

The law – your teacher will tell you the correct laws to write down.

birth _____	birth _____
1 _____	1 _____
2 _____	2 _____
3 _____	3 _____
4 _____	4 _____
5 _____	5 _____
6 _____	6 _____
7 _____	7 _____
8 _____	8 _____
9 _____	9 _____
10 _____	10 _____
11 _____	11 _____
12 _____	12 _____
13 _____	13 _____
14 _____	14 _____
15 _____	15 _____
16 _____	16 _____
17 _____	17 _____
18 _____	18 _____
19 _____	19 _____
20 _____	20 _____
21 _____	21 _____
22 _____	22 _____
23 _____	23 _____

Booze words

The language of alcohol

AIMS

To ensure the pupils know the meaning of words associated with alcohol.

Teaching Points

- ◆ Pupils need to understand words associated with alcohol and types of alcohol. Some of the words should be explained.
- ◆ Examples of names for alcoholic drinks: booze, bevvy, wine, beer, champagne, cider, real ale, spirits, alcopops, meths, ethyl alcohol, names of specific spirits, brand names, names of mixtures, mixers, cocktails.
- ◆ Examples of names for drinkers: boozer, wino, drunk, 'one of the lads', alcoholic.
- ◆ Examples of other words associated with alcohol: pub, off-licence, drunk, intoxicated, boozer, plastered, paralytic, sozzled, merry, legless, tipsy.

USING THE ACTIVITY SHEET

The focus of the activity is to find out what words associated with alcohol the pupils know and to ensure that they understand them.

Step 1   Explain to everyone in the class that you want to check their understanding of words associated with alcohol. Hand out the activity sheet, to be completed individually.

Step 2   Divide the pupils into small groups and give each group an additional sheet. Ask them to combine and sort their words on the first notice into different types of drink, for example wines, spirits and so on. Make a combined list on the board to check, correct and extend their knowledge. Do the same with the second notice using the headings 'negative', 'positive' and 'neutral' words.

Step 3   Use a similar approach for the words on the third notice, ensuring they know what the words mean, for example the difference between an off-licence and a pub, and the subtle differences in the range of words used for being under the influence of alcohol.

Step 4   Ask the pupils, working individually, to look at all the words and note on their activity sheets one thing they have learned about each of the three different areas. They may feed this back if they wish.

Extension Activities

- ◆ Suggest that the pupils go through two magazines for different audiences, listing and counting the words associated with alcohol that are used. They can present the information in graph form.
- ◆ Ask the pupils to conduct a survey of friends and family on some of the words they use about alcohol and their definitions. They should look the words up in a dictionary and compare the definitions.

Outcomes

- ◆ An understanding of a range of terms about alcohol and drinkers.
- ◆ An awareness that the same words may have varying meanings and connotations to different people.
- ◆ The development of collating and comparing skills.

Booze words

Notice 1 – names for alcoholic drinks

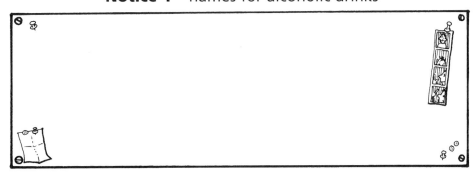

Notice 2 – names for drinkers

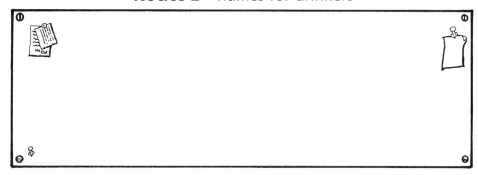

Notice 3 – other words associated with alcohol

At the end of the lesson, look at all the words that the class has generated and make a note of one thing you have learned about each of the three different areas.

1. Names for alcoholic drinks _____

_____

2. Names for drinkers _____

_____

3. Other words associated with alcohol _____

_____

Under the influence

The short-term effects of alcohol

AIMS

To ensure that the pupils understand the short-term effects of alcohol.

Teaching Points

◆ Drinking alcohol affects the body, the mind and the behaviour of the drinker.
◆ Drinking will take effect slowly and take some time to wear off.
◆ Nothing can stop the effects of intoxication, except time.
◆ The effects of drinking alcohol vary according to a range of factors: the strength of the drink, how quickly it is drunk, how much is drunk, how much food is in the stomach, the body-weight of the drinker, their personality and surroundings, and how much the person is used to drinking.

USING THE ACTIVITY SHEET

The focus of the activity is to draw out what the pupils think the short-term effects of alcohol are and to inform them of the reality.

Step 1 Hand out the activity sheets. On the first outline, ask the pupils to mark each of the short-term effects of alcohol.

Step 2 Draw a similar outline on the board. Using feedback from the class, mark this with everything on their outline, without comment.

Step 3 Draw a second outline on the board. Read the following, marking each effect on the outline as you do so for the pupils to copy.

'When alcohol is drunk it goes from the stomach to the bloodstream. The effects start after five or ten minutes and can last for several hours, depending on how much is drunk.

Most people become more relaxed when they drink a small amount of alcohol. They may do and say things they would not normally say and do. Some may become happier, others more aggressive. As people drink more they may lose control of their bodies. They may also slur their words. They might even fall over, have double vision or become unconscious.'

Step 4 Ask them to write on their sheets what factors vary the effects of drinking alcohol. Obtain feedback from the class. Compare their opinions with the information in the teaching points.

Extension Activities

◆ A selection of alcohol education videos is available from BBC Education. This includes (from the school television series *Turning Points*) a programme about alcohol misuse.
◆ Ask the pupils to design a poster or information sheet to include the positive and negative effects of drinking alcohol.

Outcomes

◆ An understanding of the short-term effects of drinking alcohol and the factors that vary its effect.

Under the influence

1. Mark what you think are the short-term effects of drinking alcohol on the first body outline.

2. Leave the second one blank. Your teacher will tell you what to do with it.

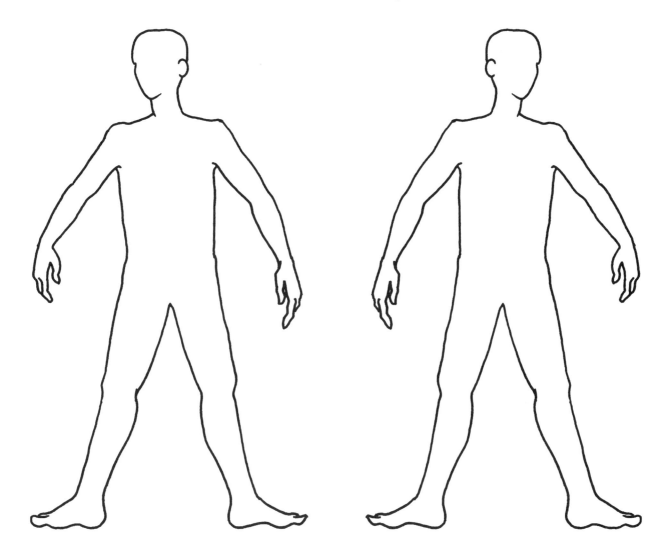

3. What factors will vary the effects of drinking alcohol?

_____

_____

_____

_____

_____

_____

On the bottle

The long-term effects of alcohol

AIMS

To ensure that the pupils understand the long-term effects of alcohol.

Teaching Points

◆ Drinking too much alcohol every day is likely to lead to dependence.
◆ Physical dependence is when the body needs alcohol to function normally.
◆ Psychological dependence is when alcohol is drunk daily for stimulation, pleasure or escape.
◆ Alcohol supplies calories, but no other dietary essentials, so heavy drinking may encourage obesity and inadequate diet, which may lead to stomach and liver disorders and brain damage.
◆ Excessive drinking may aggravate family, personal and financial problems, or induce violence and crime associated with loss of control.
◆ Suddenly stopping heavy drinking produces sweating, anxiety, trembling and delirium (the DT's), and can even result in convulsions, coma and death.
◆ Women drinking six units (see Activity 9 – Teacher's notes) or more a day may give birth to babies that are underweight, suffering from withdrawal symptoms or developmentally retarded.

USING THE ACTIVITY SHEET

The focus of this activity is to compare what the pupils think are the long-term effects of heavy drinking with the real effects.

Step 1   Hand out the activity sheets and divide the pupils into small groups. Ask them to write on the bottle outline what they think the effects of heavy drinking over a long period of time are, putting the physical effects inside the outline and other effects outside it.

Step 2   Draw a similar bottle on the board. Ask each group in turn for one effect. If it is correct, add it to the drawing and ask all the groups to put a circle around it if it appears on their drawing. When all the suggestions have been written on the board, ask the pupils to copy and circle the suggestions that are missing on their activity sheet.

Step 3   Ask the pupils to write down the reasons why someone might drink heavily over a long period of time. Ask the class for feedback and discuss possible reasons, for example relationship problems, teenage depression, stress and so on.

Step 4   Ask the pupils to compare this accurate information with what they entered on their outline and to note, and perhaps share, one thing they have learned.

Extension Activities

◆ Ask the pupils to consider the portrayal of alcoholics on television and in films. Why do they drink, and what are the effects of this drinking?
◆ Discuss with the pupils the similarities and differences between people who are dependent on alcohol, cigarettes and illegal drugs.

Outcomes

◆ An understanding of the long-term effects of heavy drinking, both physical and social.
◆ Some awareness of the reasons why a person might start, and continue, to drink heavily.

On the bottle

1. What do you think the effects of heavy drinking over a long period of time are? Write the physical effects inside the outline and other effects outside it.

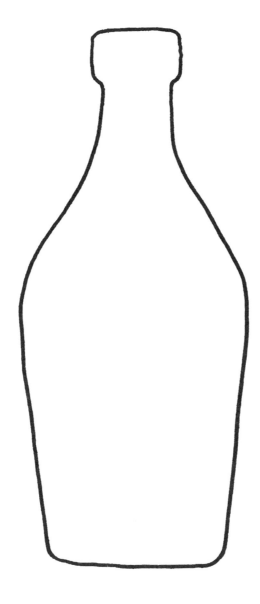

2. Why might someone drink heavily over a long period of time?

_____

_____

_____

_____

_____

_____

Strong stuff

The strengths of alcoholic drinks

AIMS

To ensure the pupils understand that alcoholic drinks vary in strength.

Teaching Points

- The amount of alcohol in a drink varies according to the type of drink.
- Alcoholic drink containers have an indication of their strength on them. The alcohol by volume (ABV) is printed as a percentage.
- In general, the order of alcoholic strength of drinks, starting from the strongest, is: spirits, fortified wine, wine, strong beers, alcopops, standard beers.
- The ABV of these types of drink is: spirits 37+%, fortified wine 15–20%, wine 10–13%, strong beers 4.5–10%, alcopops 4–5.5%, standard beers 3–4.5%.

USING THE ACTIVITY SHEET

The focus of this activity is to correct the pupils' understanding of the relative alcoholic strengths of different drinks.

Step 1   Hand out the activity sheets and ask the pupils, working individually, to order the drinks listed on the sheet according to strength. Share answers with the class and try to come to a class consensus. Tell them the correct order and ask them to copy it in the appropriate place on the activity sheet.

Step 2   Explain that all alcoholic drinks have a percentage figure on them that indicates how much alcohol they contain by volume (ABV). Ask them, working individually, to consider and write down what the ABV percentage is in each drink and try to come to a class consensus.

Tell them the correct percentages and ask them to complete the appropriate section on the activity sheet.

Step 3   Ask them to write the types of drink and ABV percentage in order next to the glasses and to shade in the appropriate amount of alcohol for each type of drink.

Step 4   Ask them to consider what they have learned in this lesson and how they will use the information in future.

Extension Activities

- Ask pupils to note the ABV percentage of a variety of drinks in a supermarket. Present the data using appropriate diagrams and graphs.
- Ask pupils to watch their favourite soap for a week and note which drinks, alcoholic and non-alcoholic, two of the characters have. They could write a humorous poem including the information that they have collected.

Outcomes

- A general understanding of the variation of the alcoholic strength of different drinks.
- Specific knowledge of the alcoholic strength of individual types of drinks.
- Some understanding of percentage in relation to volume.

Strong stuff

1. From the list below, put the types of drink in order of strength, starting with the strongest.

   Alcopops, fortified wine (port, sherry), standard beers, strong beers, spirits, wine.

	Your order	Correct order	Your %	Correct %
1				
2				
3				
4				
5				
6				

2. How much alcohol do you think is in each drink from the list above? Write the name of each drink in order of strength and its ABV percentage next to the glass and shade in the percentage of alcohol.

100%

10%

Unit-ed

Units of alcohol explained

AIMS

To ensure that the pupils understand what a unit of alcohol is and how to use the concept.

Teaching Points

◆ One unit of alcohol is the amount that will be processed in one hour by an average adult.
◆ Some drinks manufacturers now label their products with the number of units contained within them.
◆ The number of units of alcohol in a drink can be calculated by multiplying the volume of the drink in millilitres by the ABV percentage and dividing the result by 1000. For example, the number of units in a 330ml bottle of lager at 5% ABV, is 330 times 5, divided by 1000 = 1.7 units.
◆ Only time can reduce the effect of alcohol.
◆ Healthy limits for adults are 3–4 units per day for a man and 2–3 units for a woman.
◆ Healthy limits for a week are 28 units for a man and 21 units for a woman.

USING THE ACTIVITY SHEET

The focus of the activity is to develop an understanding of units of alcohol and the time taken to process them.

Step 1   Ask the pupils if they have heard of units of alcohol and what this means. Explain and hand out the activity sheet.

Step 2   Ask the pupils to calculate the total number of units in the 'rounds'. Provide them with the answers (A is 6 units, B is 5 units and C is 11 units).

Step 3   Ask the pupils to work out when the two drinkers will be completely sober and then tell them the correct answers. (Units of alcohol can only be processed one at a time, and therefore the hour for processing each unit has to follow that for the previous one. Terry will be completely sober at 7pm, Alison at 6am.)

Step 4   Ask the pupils what they believe are regarded as healthy limits for drinking alcohol. Tell them the correct limits, but ensure that they understand that these are for adults and not for young people.

Extension Activities

◆ Ask each pupil to devise his or her own scenario similar to those used in Activity 9. The scenarios should be presented to the class and the class asked to supply answers.
◆ Ask the pupils to examine drinks at home or in a supermarket and note the volume of drink in the container and the ABV percentage. The pupils could calculate the units of alcohol in each container where this is not provided.

Outcomes

◆ An understanding of units of alcohol, including how long alcohol may affect a drinker.
◆ An understanding of healthy limits for an adult drinking alcohol.

Unit-ed

A unit of alcohol is the amount that an average person can process in one hour.

The following drinks contain about one unit of alcohol:

one single pub measure of spirit	one small glass of wine	half a pint of ordinary strength beer (3.6%), lager or cider	one small glass of sherry

1. How many units of alcohol are there in these 'rounds'?

   A. Two pints of beer, a glass of wine and a sherry = _____ units.
   B. A pint of lager, a double whisky, a half of cider and three lemonades = _____ units.
   C. Five glasses of wine, three rum and cokes and three halves of lager = _____ units.

2. At what time will these two people be completely sober?

   A. Terry has a pint of beer at 1pm, another with his lunch at 1.30pm and a third just before he goes back to work at 2pm. He will be completely sober at _____ .

   B. Alison has a glass of wine at 7pm, another at 7.15pm and a third at 7.30pm. She goes out and has a pint of lager at 8pm, another at 9pm and a third at 10pm. She finishes off the evening with a double vodka at 11pm. She will be completely sober at

   _____ .

3. What do you think are the healthy limits that the Government suggests for men and women to drink in a day and in a week?

   Men per day   _____ units.
   Men per week   _____ units.
   Women per day   _____ units.
   Women per week   _____ units.

Drinking rules OK?

The acceptability of drinking on specific occasions

——— AIMS ———

To develop an understanding that the acceptability of drinking varies with the occasion.

Teaching Points

◆ It may be appropriate for young people to drink alcohol on some occasions and not on others.
◆ This may vary according to the place, the time, the people, the alcoholic drinks and any explicit or implicit conditions associated with the situation.
◆ Young people need to be aware of their personal and social responsibility in making these decisions.
◆ Your views on this may be different from the pupils' and their families'.
◆ Cultural considerations will be important in this respect.

——— USING THE ACTIVITY SHEET ———

The focus of the activity is to consider the appropriateness of drinking alcohol on a variety of occasions and to generate 'rules' that the pupils can apply to situations in which they may be involved.

Step 1 Ask the class to describe real or fictional situations in which someone their age has drunk alcohol and it has been either appropriate or not. Hand out the activity sheets and ask the pupils to select two scenarios from their sheet, one that makes up an acceptable drinking situation and the other unacceptable, in terms of the effects on the drinker or on others.

Step 2 In small groups, ask the pupils to discuss their scenarios, with the task of developing general statements about the acceptability of drinking, for example, 'It's OK to drink alcohol if your parents offer it to you.'

Step 3 Share the group statements, one per group to start with, and negotiate a class set of drinking rules, for example, 'If you are unsure whether it is appropriate for you to drink, ask a suitable adult.'

Step 4 Ask the groups, randomly, to make up situations from the list on the activity sheet and apply the drinking rules to them.

Extension Activities

◆ Ask the pupils to write a scenario, to include a discussion after the event, between a drinker and someone who regarded their drinking as inappropriate.
◆ Ask the class to choose a hypothetical family or social situation they may be involved with in the future, and write down exactly how they might apply the rules.

Outcomes

◆ An understanding of the appropriateness of drinking alcohol in a variety of situations.
◆ Negotiation and assertiveness skills.
◆ Some understanding of the need to think ahead and plan for some situations.

Drinking rules OK?

Choose one factor from each list to make up a situation in which the drinking is acceptable and one in which it is not. You may add your own factors.

People: boy your age, girl your age, boy younger than you, girl younger than you, boy older than you, girl older than you, single male adult, single female adult, married male adult, married female adult, grandparent.

Drinks: one shandy, a pint of beer, a sherry, a bottle of cider, a spirit (pub measure), spirit with mixer (for example, rum and blackcurrant or a gin and tonic), a variety of different drinks over a period of time, champagne, enough of any drink(s) to get 'tipsy' or drunk, a non-alcoholic drink.

Occasions: meal at home, meal at a restaurant, teenager's party, adult party, wedding, funeral, birth celebration, evening out, picnic or any similar occasion.

Reasons: to be sociable, to try something, to get drunk, to do what others are doing, as a dare, to enhance the situation, to celebrate.

1. Appropriate drinking situation.

2. Inappropriate drinking situation.

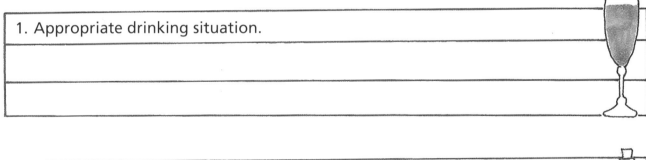

3. Now consider the effects of drinking on these occasions on the drinker and on others.

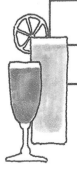

4. With other members of your group, develop three general statements about the appropriateness of drinking on a variety of occasions. Use the back of the sheet to write down your statements.

Drink with attitude

Attitudes of different people to drinkers and non-drinkers

AIMS

To explore the range of attitudes towards drinkers and drinking.

Teaching Points

Materials needed
A selection of magazine and newspaper articles and advertisements involving alcohol.

◆ There is a wide range of attitudes that different people have towards alcohol and to those who drink it.
◆ These attitudes may be affected by the law, morals, personal experience, concern for the welfare of the drinker or other factors and information received.
◆ People's attitudes will also have an effect upon their own behaviour and how they deal with other people.

USING THE ACTIVITY SHEET

The focus of the activity is to develop a scene that shows the reasons why people might have particular attitudes to drinkers and drinking.

Step 1   Ask the class for examples of what people's opinions about drinking may be and the reasons they may have them.

Step 2   Make a class collection of stories, articles or advertisements involving alcohol in newspapers and magazines.

Step 3   Ask pupils to choose two sources to use with their activity. Hand out the activity sheets and ask pupils to examine the contents of each, writing down the attitudes towards alcohol and the reasons behind them for each one.

Step 4   Pupils can attach their sources to either side of the sheets and present their ideas

to the class. These may also be used to form a class display.

Step 5   Discuss the range of attitudes expressed, the reasons for them and any development of the pupils' views.

Extension Activities

◆ Ask pupils to choose two magazines with different audiences and compare the types of drinks and images in their alcohol adverts.
◆ Ask each pupil to select a TV character who drinks or does not drink alcohol. They should make a list of the reasons for the character's attitude towards drinking and other characters' attitudes towards them.

Outcomes

◆ Increased awareness of the range of attitudes towards drinkers and drinking and the reasons for them.
◆ An understanding that people's attitudes to alcohol, or anything else, are based on a range of experience and information.
◆ Developing skills in analysing and comparing.

Drink with attitude

1. Find two stories, articles or advertisements involving alcohol in newspapers and magazines. Write down the attitudes towards alcohol and the possible reasons behind them in these two boxes.

Source 1 _____

Attitudes towards alcohol:

_____

_____

_____

_____

Reasons behind the attitudes:

_____

_____

_____

_____

Source 2 _____

Attitudes towards alcohol:

_____

_____

_____

_____

Reasons behind the attitudes:

_____

_____

_____

_____

2. Now compare the two sources. How do their attitudes differ and why?

_____

_____

_____

_____

_____

_____

_____

_____

_____

_____

Media messages

Media presentations of alcohol

— AIMS —

To explore how media portrayals of drinkers and drinking affect young people.

Teaching Points

◆ Media portrayals of drinkers and drinking may be included for the dramatic effect or may be an unsensational part of a character's life.
◆ Either may have an effect or influence on young people.

USING THE ACTIVITY SHEET

The focus of the activity is to consider the effects that media scenes or stories about alcohol have on the pupils.

Step 1   Hand out the activity sheets. Ask the pupils to note a range of scenes and situations involving alcohol from television, film, newspapers and magazines (not advertisements). Tell them that you will be asking them to write about one of these situations, particularly in relation to the effect it had on them.

Step 2   Negotiate roughly equal numbers of pupils to describe the scenes and stories they remember from the categories of television, film, newspapers and magazines. Ask pupils to write their chosen story, or describe their scene, on the activity sheet.

They need to list the possible effects on someone their age, to underline the actual effects it had on them and to note the elements that produced the effect.

Step 3   Make class lists of the elements that had positive and negative effects on the pupils and order them according to popularity. Discuss whether they reinforce or change their information, views and behaviour.

Step 4   Ask the pupils to adapt their story or scene to have a different effect, and share their changes with a partner.

Extension Activities

◆ Ask the pupils to compare two examples of alcohol portrayal in the media, one of which is 'idealistic' and one of which is 'realistic'. They should consider factors such as cost, image and health.
◆ Ask the pupils to search for the topics 'alcohol' and 'young people' on the Internet. Once they have found an interesting website they could write a one paragraph review of it.

Outcomes

◆ An understanding that media presentations involving alcohol may reinforce or change people's views.
◆ A simple approach to deconstructing a media item, which may make pupils aware of techniques designed to have specific effects.
◆ Developing skills of evaluating and comparing.

Media messages

1. Write under the drawing a list of scenes or situations involving alcohol that you remember seeing. Do not include advertisements.

TV   film   newspaper   magazine

2. Describe the one you have chosen.

_____

_____

_____

_____

3. List the possible effects it might have on a young person.

_____

_____

_____

_____

4. Underline the effects it had on you.

5. Rewrite it to have a different effect on you.

_____

_____

_____

_____

Booze for you, sir?

Alcohol advertising

AIMS

To alert pupils to the techniques used to persuade people to buy alcohol.

Teaching Points

Materials needed
A range of magazine advertisements.

◆ Advertisers use a range of techniques and images to persuade people to buy alcohol and other drinks.
◆ Attitudes to alcohol and specific drinks may be reinforced or developed by advertising.
◆ The voluntary code for advertising alcohol states that advertisements should not:
  – encourage excessive drinking
  – be directed at under 18s through style of presentation, content or context
  – feature characters who appeal to under 18s to encourage them to drink
  – suggest that any alcoholic drink can enhance mental, physical or sexual capabilities, popularity, attractiveness, masculinity, femininity or sporting achievements
  – portray drinking as promoting success in a personal relationship or social event
  – portray alcohol as a challenge, nor suggest drinking is brave, tough or daring.

USING THE ACTIVITY SHEET

The focus of the activity is to design an advert for a drink, to consider its effect on young people and its compliance with the advertising code.

Step 1   Discuss with the class how advertisements from magazines and television try to persuade their audience (using the senses, image etc.).

Step 2   Hand out the activity sheets and ask the pupils, individually, or in pairs, to design an advert for a fictitious drink (additional A4 sheets of paper may be needed). Ensure that TV and printed media adverts for both alcoholic and soft drinks are covered. Ask the pupils to list the elements intended to appeal to the audience.

Step 3   Collect and make a list of the elements intended to appeal to the audience for the alcoholic drinks and then the non-alcoholic

drinks. Compare and contrast the lists, extracting those that are for alcohol and that may have some appeal to young people.

Step 4   Ask the pupils what restrictions might be in the voluntary code for advertising alcohol, especially about young people. Compare this with the actual code.

Step 5   Ask the pupils to exchange their sheet with another pupil, or pair, with the same medium and a different kind of drink. They are to analyse and report back to the designers on: elements that appeal to them and that break the advertising code, and whether the drinks are alcoholic or not.

Extension Activities

◆ The pupils may write a fictional letter to the Advertising Standards Authority commenting on whether, and how, a TV or magazine alcohol advert breaks the advertising code.

Outcomes

◆ Some understanding of the techniques used to advertise alcoholic drinks.
◆ Knowledge of relevant aspects of the voluntary code for advertising alcohol.

Booze for you, sir?

1. Choose a target audience for your product.

2. Design an advert for a drink to be shown on TV or published in a magazine.

3. List the elements of the advert that are intended to appeal to the people who see the advert.

_____

_____

_____

_____

4. Circle the elements in the list above that conflict with the voluntary code for alcohol advertising.

Fancy a drink, kid?

Being offered a drink at home

— AIMS —

To explore situations in which a young person might be offered an alcoholic drink by a member of their family.

Teaching Points

◆ Most people start drinking alcohol in family situations with the permission of adults.
◆ It is not the intention to compare family situations and attitudes to alcohol, so request that pupils note the kinds of things that the family members might say, not verbatim versions of real conversations.
◆ Recognise that it is quite difficult for a young person to refuse an offer of an alcoholic drink from a family member if they want to.

USING THE ACTIVITY SHEET

The focus of the activity is to consider the reasons why family members might offer young people alcohol and the problems they may have in responding.

Step 1   Tell the pupils that many young people start drinking alcohol with their family; some parents use meals and other occasions to educate their children about alcohol in a safe environment.

Step 2   Choose one of the family members (parent, grandparent, uncle or aunt, older sibling) as an example and ask the class for the kind of thing that person might say when offering an alcoholic drink to a member of the family the same age as the pupils. Ask for suggestions as to how they might respond, depending on whether they accept or reject the offer, and the responses of the other person. Use a version of the speech bubbles on the activity sheet to demonstrate on the board.

Step 3   Hand out the activity sheets and ask the pupils to complete it with examples of how their family might offer them drinks, and the consequent discussions. Then ask them to answer the remaining questions on the sheet.

Step 4   Make a composite list of the answers to the questions on the board, and ask the pupils to note the two most important reasons for each response.

Extension Activities

◆ A similar activity could be carried out using examples from English literature – involving set texts if relevant.
◆ Ask the pupils to look at some examples of drinking in the home in TV soaps or in films and describe how this has particularly affected a young person.

Outcomes

◆ A greater understanding of the context of drinking in a family situation.
◆ Some consideration of how to respond to being offered alcohol by a family member, before it occurs.
◆ Evaluating the factors to take into account when offered alcohol by a family member.

Fancy a drink, kid?

1. Choose two people from parent, grandparent, uncle or aunt, older sibling, as examples of someone who might offer you an alcoholic drink. Write in the first speech bubble what they might say, in the next two what your answer might be (choose 'yes' or 'no'), and lastly how they might respond to your answer.

2. Why might members of your family offer you an alcoholic drink? List the reasons.

_____

_____

3. Why might you accept the drink?

_____

_____

4. Why might you reject the offer?

_____

_____

5. Why might the person respond the way they do?

_____

_____

6. Circle the two most important reasons for each of the above, or add them on the back of the sheet.

Friendly firewater

What do you do when your friends offer you a drink?

AIMS

To consider the factors to take into account when offered a drink by friends.

Teaching Points

◆ Decisions to drink with friends are often made very quickly and without much thought.

◆ These decisions may only be based on a few relevant and short-term factors, not necessarily those important to adults. This activity may broaden pupils' thinking in advance of such situations.

◆ Girls are more likely to be drinking at an earlier age than boys and they may have more experience and a more mature attitude to drinking.

USING THE ACTIVITY SHEET

The focus of this activity is to use specific situations to alert the pupils to the varied importance of factors affecting their decisions to drink with friends.

Step 1   Tell the class that there are likely to be lots of factors that affect young people's responses to drinking with their friends. Hand out the activity sheets and go through the first situation, using the pupils' input, adding any factors they miss out that you think are relevant.

Step 2   Ask the pupils to complete the other two situations, noting the factors that would affect their decision, putting them on the see-saw according to how important they are and indicating their decision about drinking.

Step 3   Draw the see-saw on the board and ask members of the class to suggest some factors that would affect an individual's decision to drink with friends, giving their relative 'weight' (from 1 to 5). Ask them what other factors would move it in either direction. Ensure the gender factor is raised.

Step 4   Ask the pupils to order all the factors that have been discussed in this activity from most to least important.

Extension Activities

◆ In small groups, ask the pupils to role-play some of the scenarios in the activity and discuss with others in the class how the balance of factors might change.

◆ Ask pupils to consider and write down what position they will be in, ten years from now. What factors in their life then will affect their decisions to drink with their friends?

Outcomes

◆ Some understanding of the influence of peers with regard to drinking alcohol.

◆ An approach to help analyse and prepare for drinking with friends.

◆ Developing skills in prioritising and evaluating.

Friendly firewater

For each of the situations below, write the factors in the boxes on the left-hand side that may persuade you to drink. In the boxes on the right, write those that may stop you. Number the boxes and draw smaller ones on the see-saw; the ones that are more likely to affect you go furthest away from the balance point. Circle 'yes' or 'no' according to the balance of the factors.

1. You are alone in your house with friends of your own gender, but mostly older than you, and one takes a large bottle of cider out of a bag and offers it around.

YES   NO

2. You are in someone else's house with friends who are of both genders. The parents are getting ready to go out and they have left open bottles of wine and spirits in the room where you and your friends are. The friend who lives in the house suggests everybody takes a drink each from one of the bottles, before the parents come down to go out.

YES   NO

3. You are in a park with friends who are all of the opposite sex. One takes a pack of high strength beer out of their bag and suggests that you all try to get drunk as quickly as possible.

YES   NO

4. List all the factors that would affect whether you take a drink from a friend, from the most important to the least important. Use the back of the sheet for your answers.

Be sociable

Being offered a drink on social occasions

─── AIMS ───

To consider responses to young people being offered alcohol on formal occasions.

Teaching Points

◆ Young people may not be totally aware of conventions with regard to drinking in more formal situations.
◆ Sharing your past experience, both as a young person and as an adult, may be helpful in this activity.

─── USING THE ACTIVITY SHEET ───

The focus of the activity is to highlight the choices available to young people when they are offered alcohol.

Step 1 Tell the pupils that you are going to consider more formal social situations in which young people may be offered alcohol. Hand out the activity sheets and ask the pupils to select one of the scenarios. Try to ensure that they do not all choose the same one.

Step 2 Ask the pupils to complete the task on their own and then to compare responses in pairs or small groups. See if they can find some general problems about accepting drinks in more formal situations (e.g. you may upset some people by refusing a drink and other people by taking it, or you may be affected by the alcohol in something like champagne, which you are not used to).

Step 3 Collect and list the general problems on the board and then ask for, and write up, suggestions for overcoming them.

Step 4 Ask the pupils, in their small groups, to relate a recent experience of drinking at a more formal occasion and to look ahead to ones they may be involved with. They should consider how they could use the suggestions for overcoming the problems.

Extension Activities

◆ Ask the pupils to compile lists, individually or in groups, of the positive and negative consequences of accepting or rejecting the offer of a drink in one of the scenarios on the activity sheet.
◆ Ask the pupils to write a story in which someone decides to accept a drink and then goes back in time and changes their mind, emphasising how their decision affects events.

Outcomes

◆ An understanding of some of the subtleties and conventions associated with young people drinking in formal situations.
◆ Some strategies to employ to overcome the problems in these situations.
◆ Recognising personal responsibility in making decisions in a social context.

Be sociable

Select one of the following events and answer the questions.

A. You are at a birthday party for one of your parents at your house. One of their friends offers you a drink when your parents haven't.

B. You are at a wedding and the waiter offers you wine with the meal, champagne for the toast and a drink from the free bar at the end of the meal.

C. You are having your first meal at your boyfriend's or girlfriend's house. The father offers you a glass of wine with a wink in his eye.

Questions

1. What do you think the person is thinking when offering you a drink?

_____

_____

_____

2. What would you be thinking when they offer you a drink?

_____

_____

_____

3. How do you think other people who are there or not there (for example, parents or friends) would expect you to respond?

_____

_____

_____

4. In a small group, list the general problems that may have to be dealt with in situations like these. Use the back of the sheet and add solutions when the teacher tells you to.

_____

_____

_____

Bottled out

The risks of drinking alcohol

AIMS

To consider the risks associated with different levels of drinking.

Teaching Points

The risks of drinking:
◆ a small amount of alcohol include saying and doing things you would not normally say or do, for example talking to people in authority inappropriately, responding to 'dares', becoming aggressive, taking other drugs, having less coordination and control, or taking the risk of breaking the law.
◆ a lot of alcohol in one session include all of the above to an increased proportion. It can also promote slurring of speech, not knowing what you are doing, exaggerated and variable emotional reactions, vomiting, accidents caused by lack of control, double vision, loss of balance, unconsciousness or not remembering what you did.
◆ large amounts of alcohol every day, leading to dependency, include obesity, nutrient deficiencies, stomach and liver disorders, and family, personal and financial problems. There is the risk that women may give birth to smaller babies. Withdrawal symptoms when drinking is stopped can lead to sweating, anxiety, trembling and delirium, convulsions, coma and death.

USING THE ACTIVITY SHEET

The focus of the activity is to elicit the risks associated with drinking alcohol and to consider whether the risks are worth taking.

Step 1   Hand out the activity sheets and ask the pupils to draw, or write in the bottles, some risks associated with drinking a little, a lot in one session, and every day, without discussion.

Step 2   Divide the class into small groups and ask them to combine their lists of risks on an additional sheet and rank them from low risk to high risk.

Step 3   Ask the groups to consider what makes some of the risks worth taking and how they can avoid the risks they do not want to take. Discuss this with the whole class, adding some of the risks from the teaching points that they have not mentioned.

Step 4   Ask them to write, on the back of their sheets, why they would take, or avoid, each risk they have listed.

Extension Activities

◆ Ask the pupils to consider the risks in another activity they will be involved with in the next week, for example learning new skills, social situations and so on. Ask them to decide which risks are worth taking.
◆ Instruct the pupils to write a newspaper report in which someone took a risk with alcohol.

Outcomes

◆ Greater awareness of personal responsibility towards risk taking.
◆ Specific understanding of the risks associated with drinking alcohol.
◆ A simple approach to risk assessment.

Bottled out

1. Draw or write in the bottles the risks associated with drinking alcohol.

a little　　　　**a lot in one session**　　　　**every day**

2. In your group, order the risks from high to low.

High _____

_____

_____

_____

_____

_____

Low _____

3. On the back of the sheet, write why you would take, or avoid, each risk you have listed.

Drink talking

Discussing a drink problem with different people

AIMS

To explore different people's reactions to a young person's concerns about drinking.

Teaching Points

Materials needed

It might be useful to find out about your local youth and drug and alcohol counselling agency before this lesson, particularly the details of how they work.

National telephone helpline numbers that might be useful are Drinkline 0800 917 8282 and Childline 0800 1111.

You and the pupils need to be aware of the school policy and procedures, including confidentiality and referral issues, with regard to disclosure.

USING THE ACTIVITY SHEET

The focus of the activity is to highlight key issues facing young people with drinking problems and how these might be addressed.

Step 1   Explain that a small number of young people have drink problems and may have difficulty talking about them. Hand out the activity sheets and ask the pupils to complete them, working individually.

Step 2   Divide the class into groups of four. Ask the pupils to choose one of their conversations to present to the class. Try to ensure that there is one group for each example. Ask them to decide why there is a difference between what is expected and what is wanted from the listener.

Step 3   Ask them to present their conversations; three pupils should say the parts and the fourth should explain the difference. Discuss each presentation before moving on to the next one. Try to draw out any generalisations, about both the disclosure and the response.

Step 4   Ask the groups to consider what both young people and relevant adults could do to make appropriate discussion of problem drinking easier. Ask them to feed this back and make a list of suggestions on the board.

Extension Activities

◆ Ask pupils to find out about your local youth and drug and alcohol counselling agency and national helplines both for young people and for alcohol problems. Results could be presented on a public information sheet (the ICT Department could be involved).

◆ Invite a guest speaker from a local agency to come in and talk to the pupils.

Outcomes

◆ An understanding of how the school and other agencies may be able to help young people experiencing problems with alcohol.

◆ Some understanding of the difficulties that people may have in talking about drinking problems to other people.

◆ Developing skills in listening and empathising.

Drink talking

1. Choose three of the following: friend, teacher, parent or carer, doctor, youth worker or telephone helpline. For each of them, write in the first speech bubble what you might say to them if you had a concern about your own or someone else's drinking, in the second one how you would expect them to respond and in the third one how you would like them to respond.

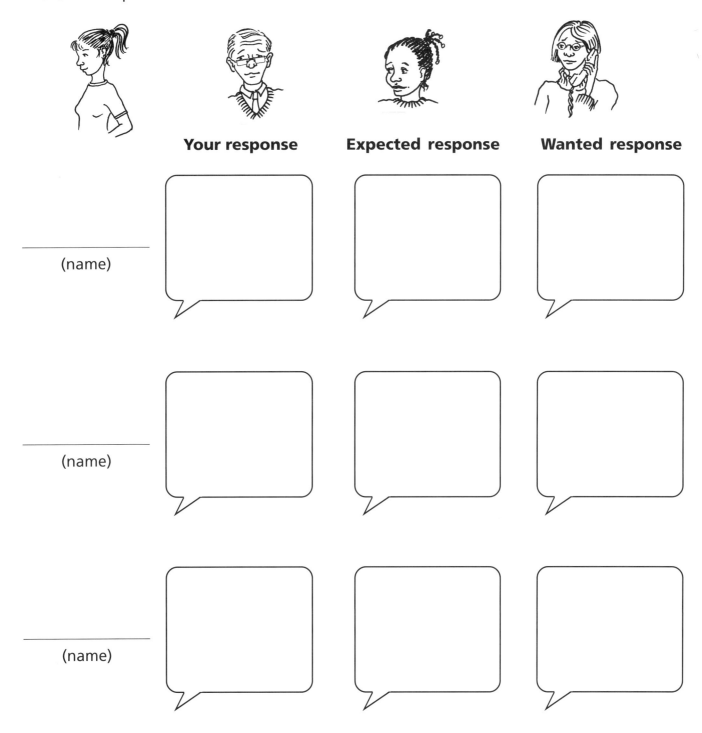

Your response   **Expected response**   **Wanted response**

_____ (name)

_____ (name)

_____ (name)

2. On the back of the sheet, write down what young people and relevant adults could do to make discussion about drinking problems easier.

Help!

Assisting a friend under the influence

AIMS

To alert pupils to simple and appropriate action to take in order to help someone who is drunk.

Teaching Points

- People who are drunk may not be able, or may not want, to do what is best for them.
- Do not administer first aid unless you are absolutely sure of what you are doing. Find out from a trained first aider exactly what the current recommended recovery position is.
- The best thing to do is to seek help from a responsible and sober adult.
- The health and safety of the person is more important than whether you think anyone will get into trouble.
- If the person is unwell and you are asked what they have been drinking, be completely honest.
- Coffee will not help someone sober up, only time can do this.

USING THE ACTIVITY SHEET

The focus of the activity is to generate an awareness of responsibility towards the safety of a drunk person, including some appropriate action to take.

Step 1 Tell the pupils that it is possible that they will be in the presence of friends under the influence of drink who may need some help. Ask if anyone has been in that situation, but don't ask for any details (yet). Hand out the activity sheet and ask the pupils to complete the first column individually.

Step 2 In pairs, or small groups, ask them to compare their lists and then to complete the second column together. Take feedback from the groups and list the most common problems on the board.

Step 3 Ask them how these problems might affect what they want to do for their friend. Lead the discussion towards consideration of the safest and simplest things to do (see teaching points, which could be written on the board at this point).

Step 4 Ask the groups to consider their original suggestions in the first column and to tick the appropriate ones and to cross out those that are inappropriate. They then need to copy what is on the board.

Extension Activities

- In small groups, ask the pupils to develop a scene in which someone tries to help a drunken friend. Ask them to 'rewind' and go through the scene with a different action and outcome. (No fights or deaths!)
- Ask the pupils to write a newspaper report of an incident in which someone their age was praised for their action in helping a drunken friend.

Outcomes

- An understanding of the difficulties of dealing with someone who is drunk.
- Some understanding of the appropriate action to take when dealing with someone who is drunk.
- Developing skills in prioritising and problem-solving.

Help!

<table>
<tr><td>

1. Things to do to help a drunk friend:

_____

_____

_____

_____

_____

_____

_____

_____

_____

_____

</td><td>

2. Problems dealing with a drunk friend:

_____

_____

_____

_____

_____

_____

_____

_____

_____

_____

</td></tr>
</table>

3. Tick the appropriate actions and cross out those that are inappropriate, then copy what is on the board into the box below.

1. _____

2. _____

3. _____

4. _____

5. _____

6. _____

7. _____

Drink, drink, drink ...

Coping with long-term problems

— AIMS —

To alert pupils to some of the elements of long-term problems associated with drinking and to how people can best respond.

Teaching Points

◆ People who have problems with drink tend to hide or deny it, even to themselves.
◆ You can only help someone if they accept that they have a drink problem and are willing to do something about it.
◆ Most people with drink problems are likely to have other problems that the drink seems to help them to deal with; these problems need to be dealt with first.
◆ It is not advisable to confront someone with a drink problem while they are under the influence of alcohol.
◆ In some circumstances, the best thing for a young person to do might be nothing, other than sensitively to inform appropriate people.
◆ For further information, contact Alcohol Concern, Tel: 020 7928 7377.

— USING THE ACTIVITY SHEET —

The focus of the activity is to generate the indicators and consequences of problem drinking and to consider what action the drinker and others can take.

Step 1   Tell the pupils that long-term heavy drinking can affect people physically, mentally, socially, financially, or legally (you may have to explain these terms). Hand out the activity sheet and ask the pupils to write, inside the face, the indicators of a problem drinker and, outside it, the consequences.

Step 2   Write the five problem headings (physical, mental ...) on the board, and ask the pupils, one at a time, to tell you an effect to write under the appropriate heading, giving everyone the opportunity to contribute.

Step 3   Ask the pupils to suggest what the drinker could do and what people close to them could do to support them. Use the teaching points to assess appropriateness. When you have a comprehensive list, ask them to copy it, the ones for the drinker inside the face, and those for others outside it.

Step 4   Ask them to circle the three most obvious and worst indicators, or consequences, on the face and the most important actions inside and outside the face.

Extension Activities

◆ Ask the pupils to write a letter about a drink problem to an agony aunt or uncle in a young person's magazine. Then ask them to exchange it with someone else and answer their letter.
◆ Ask them to write the story of someone who overcomes a drink problem with the help of a friend, from either or both people's point of view.

Outcomes

◆ Some understanding of the indicators and consequences of long-term heavy drinking.
◆ Some understanding of what problem drinkers and people close to them might do to improve the situation.

Drink, drink, drink ...

1. Write inside the face the tell-tale signs of a problem drinker and outside it the effects on the drinker and on others.

2. Copy what drinkers could do to help themselves inside the face below. Write down what people close to them could do to support them outside the face.

3. Circle what you think are the three most obvious or worst indicators, or consequences of drinking, inside the face, and the most important actions inside and outside the face.

ACTIVITY BANK: *Alcohol*

Why drink poison?

Moral and religious approaches to alcohol

AIMS

To consider how moral and religious attitudes to alcohol may contradict one another.

Teaching Points

◆ In the most orthodox Muslim countries, the Qur'an, Islam's most sacred book of scriptures, is interpreted as presenting the production and drinking of alcohol as immoral and punishable by death.
◆ A number of Christian groups insist their members be teetotal, including the Salvation Army and Seventh Day Adventists.
◆ During Prohibition in the US from 1919–1933, it was only possible to obtain alcohol legally for 'medicinal' purposes after obtaining a doctor's prescription.
◆ The drinking of alcohol is a central and symbolic act of many religious rituals and festivals, for example Catholic Mass, Jewish Passover.
◆ Alcohol is used at a variety of social occasions, for example toasts at weddings.

USING THE ACTIVITY SHEET

The focus of the activity is for pupils to consider reasons for not drinking, the groups of people who abstain, and the use of alcohol in ritual and social customs.

Step 1   Hand out the activity sheets. Ask the pupils, working individually, to list, on the left hand side of the scroll, the specific reasons why people might prefer not to drink alcohol. In small groups, ask them to compare their lists and, on the right hand side of the scroll, write headings for any reasons that are similar (e.g. moral, religious, medicinal, welfare, dietary).

Step 2   Ask the pupils to feed back these headings and write them on the board. Invite them to tell you the names they know of groups of people who don't drink alcohol, using both general words like teetotal, and specific ones like Hindus. Add any that you are aware of that they have omitted.

Step 3   In their groups, ask them to write, next to the chalice, occasions when alcohol is drunk as part of a ritual or social custom. Invite them to feed these points back, asking for clarification if necessary, and write them on the board.

Step 4   Ask the pupils, working individually, to write three sentences, using the information on the board, that clearly indicate how moral and religious attitudes to alcohol may seem to contradict one another (e.g. Seventh Day Adventists do not drink alcohol, but it is used in the Catholic Mass as a symbol of the blood of Christ). Finally, discuss with the class some possible reasons why they think these contradictions exist (e.g. different customs).

Extension Activities

◆ Invite the pupils to research two different religions' attitudes to the use of alcohol. They could refer to original texts (e.g. the Bible, the Qur'an) and ask appropriate local people.
◆ Invite the Salvation Army and a toastmaster to be involved in a debate on the use of alcohol.

Outcomes

◆ A greater understanding of different groups' attitudes towards alcohol.
◆ An understanding of the use of alcohol in rituals and social customs.

Why drink poison?

1. On the left-hand side of the scroll, write the reasons why people might prefer not to drink alcohol.

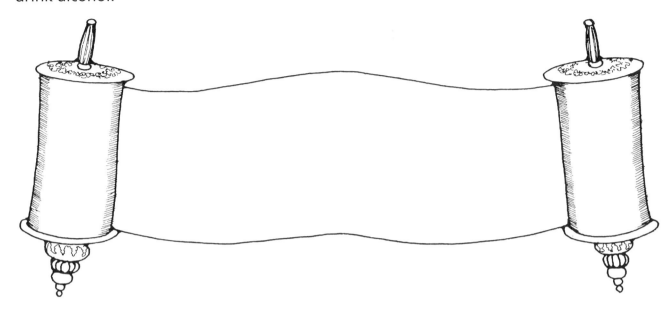

2. In small groups, write on the right-hand side of the scroll headings for reasons that are similar.

3. Write next to the chalice, occasions when alcohol is drunk as part of a ritual or social custom.

4. Write three sentences that clearly indicate the inconsistency of attitudes to alcohol.

How did you find it?

Evaluating the alcohol education lessons

— AIMS —

To evaluate the alcohol education lessons, in order to improve them for the future.

Teaching Points

Materials needed
Some extra activity sheets and some pairs of scissors.

◆ Be prepared to ask for, and receive, honest replies to the request for feedback about the alcohol education lessons.

— USING THE ACTIVITY SHEET —

The focus of the activity is for pupils to give responsible feedback about the alcohol education lessons for the purpose of their future improvement.

Step 1 Tell the pupils that you want to evaluate the alcohol education lessons so that the year-group below them can have an improved course and so that you can plan for their lessons next year and include any necessary additions. Hand out the activity sheets and ask the pupils to complete them individually.

Step 2 Divide them into groups of four and give each group an extra activity sheet. Ask the groups to combine the contents of their individual sheets on to the additional one, and then to cut up the completed composite sheet into its four parts, taking one each.

Step 3 Reorganise the class into four groups with the same part of the sheet. Ask them to combine all the information and to present it in any way they wish.

Step 4 Discuss with the class whether they thought that any activity was too hard or too easy and why.

Step 5 Ask the pupils to tell you what they thought of the process of the series of lessons; in other words, starting with asking them what they wanted covered, negotiating ground rules for discussion, involving them in the activities, and reviewing and evaluating the lessons.

Extension Activities

◆ Ask the pupils to prepare and write a short statement on one of the following:
   – in support of prohibition
   – free drinks for 11–16 year olds
   – subsidised drinking for pensioners
   – alcohol-free days
   – no tax on alcohol.
◆ Ask pupils to write a letter to the local paper telling them about their alcohol education lessons and how useful they found them.

Outcomes

◆ Evaluating the series of lessons to inform the equivalent ones for the next year-group.
◆ An understanding that the pupils' needs and views are taken into account.

How did you find it?

Write your answers in the appropriate container for each question.

1. What have you liked about it?

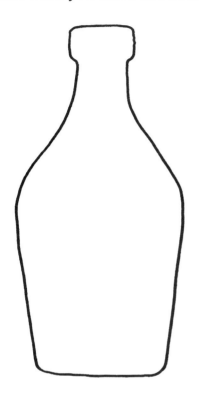

2. What was left out that might have been useful?

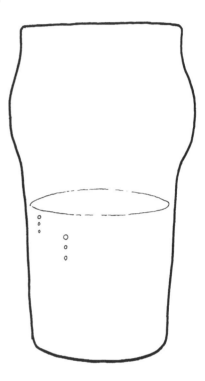

3. What should be in this course for the next year-group?

4. What should be covered for **your** group next year?

ACTIVITY BANK: *Alcohol*

Skills matrix

ACTIVITY/ SKILL	1	2	3	4	5	6	7	8	9	10	11	12	13	14	15	16	17	18	19	20	21	22
Analysing/Interpreting	●	●	●	●	●	●	●	●	●	●	●	●	●	●	●	●	●	●	●	●	●	●
Asserting			●							●												
Awareness	●	●	●	●	●	●	●	●	●	●	●		●	●	●	●	●	●	●	●	●	●
Collating	●	●	●		●							●	●			●	●					●
Communicating	●	●	●	●	●			●		●	●		●	●	●	●	●	●				●
Comparing	●	●	●	●	●	●	●	●		●	●	●	●		●	●		●	●		●	
Cooperating	●	●	●	●			●	●	●	●	●	●	●	●	●	●	●	●	●	●		●
Debating and discussing	●	●	●	●			●			●		●	●		●	●	●	●				●
Decision making			●											●	●		●					
Empathising							●							●	●			●		●		
Evaluating	●	●	●	●	●		●	●		●		●	●	●	●		●	●	●	●	●	●
Expressing (e.g. of beliefs, ideas and opinions)	●	●	●	●			●		●	●	●	●	●	●	●	●	●	●		●	●	●
ICT	●		●									●					●					
Identity and self-esteem														●	●	●						
Imagining														●	●	●		●				
Investigating	●	●	●	●	●	●		●			●	●									●	
Knowledge		●	●	●	●	●	●	●	●		●	●	●	●	●	●	●	●	●	●	●	
Listening	●	●	●	●		●	●	●	●	●		●	●	●	●	●	●	●	●	●	●	●
Negotiating										●												
Perceiving	●	●	●		●		●		●		●	●						●				●
Presenting	●				●	●		●	●		●		●				●	●	●			
Prioritising	●		●									●		●	●				●	●		
Problem solving		●												●		●		●	●	●		
Respect																		●				
Responsibility										●				●	●	●	●	●	●	●		
Understanding		●	●	●	●	●	●	●	●	●	●	●	●	●	●	●	●	●	●	●	●	●